# SHAOLIN

## Legends of Zen
## and Kung Fu

## Liow Kah Joon

SilkRoad

First Published in Canada in 2006 by SilkRoad Networks Inc.

P.O Box 25072, 50 Blvd Taschereau, Pl La Citière,

La Prairie, J5R 5H4,

Québec, Canada

With the participation of  Publishing Content Industry Development Scheme

A special Thank You to our book sponsor, Gong Ying Qi.

Refer to website: **www.living-chinese-symbols.com**

Library and Archives Canada Cataloguing in Publication

Liow, Kah Joon, 1970-
        Shaolin : legends of zen and kung fu / Liow Kah Joon.

Includes 3D animation story on DVD.
ISBN 0-9733492-3-9

1. Kung fu—Juvenile literature.  I. Title.
GV1114.7.L56 2006        j796.8159        C2006-902187-2

Illustration by Qing Xiaosong
Design by Wang Qun
Editing by Tess Johnston
Chinese calligraphy by Chen Peng, Shaolin Zen artist. To know what the Chinese characters in this book mean, see website.

Thanks to Louis, Frank and Oscar for your inspiring ideas in the creation of this book.

Printed in Hong Kong

When you come across *"see this website"* as you're reading the book, it means more stories can be found at

**www.living-chinese-symbols.com.**

# About Shaolin

Shaolin Temple in China is famous worldwide for its peaceful-looking monks who perform incredible kung fu stunts.

For a long time, I have been fascinated by the martial arts skills of Shaolin monks. How are these monks able to achieve such amazing feats?

The answer lies in Zen. Zen is the wisdom behind Shaolin and it is what makes Shaolin Kung Fu unique and powerful. In fact, the 1,500-year-old Shaolin Temple is the cradle of Zen *and* Kung Fu.

Zen is short for Zen Buddhism and is the Japanese translation of the Chinese word *Chan. (see back cover) Chan* itself is adapted from the Sanskrit word *Dhyana* which means "meditation". The word Zen is already well known outside China and I have chosen to use it instead of *Chan* for this book.

Children of all ages today love watching the on-screen kung fu stunts of Jackie Chan and Jet Li. They are also thrilled by inventive martial arts action in films such as The Matrix.

A popular Chinese saying goes "All the kung fu in the world arise from Shaolin". This book takes kids and grownups alike on a fun and exciting discovery of Shaolin Kung Fu.

Liow Kah Joon, April 2006

Beijing

Luoyang.

Shaolin

Nanjing

Guangzhou.

# What's in this Book:

# What is Zen?

A young martial artist wanted to study with a kung fu master. As the master is speaking he keeps on saying "Yes, I know that". At one point, the master pours the student tea and keeps on pouring even after the cup overflows. The student jumps up before the tea scalds him and demands to know "How can a great master spill tea like that?" The master replies, "If you wish to taste *my* tea, you must first empty *your* cup."

This story illustrates Zen -- the heart of Shaolin Kung Fu. Zen refers to an empty mind that is open to all possibilities. People who practice Zen do not think endlessly. They look and they act.

Historically, Zen is based on the teachings of the Buddha ("One Who is Awake"). The Buddha was a prince in India by the name Siddhartha Gautama 2,500 years ago. At age 29, he saw for the first time an old man, a sick man and a dead man. Deeply troubled, he gave up his luxurious life to seek a way to end suffering. Finally, after six years of meditation under a Bodhi tree, he became enlightened or free from suffering.

In *The Matrix* movie, Neo wakes up and discovers that the world around him is only an illusion. The Buddha says that the world is an illusion -- everything in it is temporary. Therefore, there's no point worrying over things. Like Neo, only when we empty our minds can we see reality and be truly happy! And the way to do it? Through Zen meditation. *(see website)*

# What is Kung Fu?

Kung fu refers in general to the wide variety of martial arts from China -- more than 1,000 styles! It should be called *gong fu* because that's how it's pronounced in Chinese Mandarin.

Kung fu and martial arts are not the same thing. Kung fu is a **skill developed through hard work** and means a very high level of martial arts ability.

In Chinese, kung fu is used outside of martial arts to refer to anyone who has achieved great skill through long practice in a chosen area.

An NBA player who gives a solid performance is said to have kung fu, as does a chef who serves up mouth-watering dishes. Even a taxi driver who's not had an accident in twenty years is said to have good kung fu! *(see website)*

# What is Shaolin Kung Fu?

A Shaolin saying goes, "Weak mind, weak fist; strong mind, no need for fist."

This short sentence offers the real purpose of Shaolin monks learning martial arts. Their goal is to develop a strong mind, *not* to achieve the highest martial arts skills.

What is a strong mind? A strong mind is compassionate. Compassion means accepting that others have a different way of seeing the world. Practicing compassion is a big part of being a Shaolin Zen monk.

A Shaolin monk avoids clashes at all costs. However, if he is attacked, a Shaolin monk merges with his opponent's energy and returns it to him. By sending back this "unwanted gift", he is saying "No" to violence!

A very strong mind is free from worry and pain. This enlightened state is the highest goal of a Shaolin monk.

(see Training at Shaolin)

# Origins of Shaolin Kung Fu

Shaolin ("young forest") is a Buddhist temple located in the Yellow River area in the heart of ancient China. It was built in 495 AD by order of the Emperor in the forests of Songshan Mountain in today's Henan province.

The Yellow River area is an important territory and warring armies fought to control it. In the eighty years after Shaolin was built, twenty emperors rose and fell. With all the fighting going on, the people suffered and many sought refuge at Shaolin Temple. Among them were warriors and generals who were excellent martial artists. They shaved their heads to become monks, and practiced and exchanged martial arts skills.

In the Song Dynasty (1,045 years ago) and Yuan Dynasty (745 years ago), the chiefs of Shaolin Temple invited the best martial artists in the land to come to Shaolin and exchange skills.

Over the years, more than 700 forms of Shaolin martial arts were created and recorded, but due to wars and fire, only more than 200 types are known today.

*(see website)*

In the legends of Shaolin, one figure towers over all others -- Damo. It was Damo who introduced zen and kung fu to Shaolin.

# Crossing The River on a Reed

About 1,500 years ago, an Indian monk by the name Bodhidharma -- or Damo as the Chinese call him -- arrived on the Southern shores of China in today's Guangzhou. *(See website for Damo's encounter with the Emperor of the South.)*

Passing through Nanjing, Damo heard a person called **Spiritual Light** (*Shen Guang*) speaking the Buddha's words to a crowd. The Indian monk listened for a while and laughed. Angered, Spiritual Light slapped him across the mouth, knocking out his front teeth. Without a word, Damo went on his way.

Soon he reached the Yangtze River. There was no boat in sight. He saw an old woman carrying a bundle of reeds and asked, "**Old woman**, could you spare me a reed so I could be on my way?" The old woman gave Damo a reed and he placed it on the water. Stepping onto the reed, he **glided across the river**.

By now, Spiritual Light knew he had made a big mistake. When he reached the river, he grabbed the old woman's bundle of reeds and jumped onto them. Immediately he sank into the water. Gasping for air, he pulled himself out of the water. "You gave him a reed and he crossed the river. I took your bundle of reeds and it sank." Spiritual Light said angrily, "Why is this so?"

Calmly the old woman replied: "He asked me for the reed politely. You robbed me of my reeds. How could I have helped you?" With that, the old woman suddenly disappeared. Spiritual Light stood on the banks alone, feeling even more sorry than before.

# Dawn of Zen and Kung Fu

After he crossed the river, Damo walked in the northerly direction until he reached Shaolin Temple. He told the Buddha's teachings to the monks, but he was shown the door. *(To know why the monks rejected Damo, and also what happened to Spiritual Light, see the website.)*

Damo retreated to a cave in the mountains overlooking Shaolin. There he sat facing a huge rock and meditated so intensely that his image was etched onto it! After nine years, the Shaolin monks decided that Damo made sense after all and invited him back to the temple as their chief.

What did Damo do in these nine years? He founded a Chinese style of Buddhism called Chan (Zen). In *Chan*, everything a person does is meditation if the person's mind is one with the task, be it washing dishes, chopping wood, sitting quietly, or training in martial arts.

Damo invented a self-defense art called *Eighteen Lohan Hands* based on the movements of animals he saw in the mountains. This he taught the Shaolin monks so they could protect themselves from wild animals and bandits. He also created *Yijinjing* or Muscle-Tendon Change Classic, a series of yoga-like movements to develop *qi* flow *(see What is Qi?)* so the monks had more energy to practice Zen.

Damo believed that physical training toughened the body and thus allowed the mind to grow stronger. A strong mind could then control a powerful body in motion. *(See website for more Zen stories.)*

**5.00 am**

*Wake up!*

**5.10 am**

*Running up and down the mountain.*

**6.30 am**

*Breakfast. Steamed tofu, vegetables, rice and soup. Rest.*

**8.00 am**

*Practice martial arts. Do chores around temple.*

**11.30 am**

*Lunch. Noodles, rice or steamed buns. Rest.*

**1.00 pm**

*More martial arts practice!*

**5.30 pm**

*Dinner. All meals are vegetarian.*

**7.00 pm**

*Read and meditate.*

**10.00 pm**

*Lights out.*

# Training At Shaolin

Students at Shaolin Temple begin training at a very early age, some as early as four years old. For six days each week, the Shaolin disciple goes through tough physical, mental and spiritual training.

Training at Shaolin involves both quiet and moving meditation. Meditation means keeping a focused mind. *(see website)*

Basic training takes as many years as is required by each student. The student studies Shaolin martial arts *(hand combat, weapons use, breath control, meditation and Qigong)* as well as Buddhist values (Avoid all evil, Do good, Purify the mind). At Shaolin, training in martial arts is a good way to learn Buddhist lessons!

In advanced training, the student might write poetry or books, paint or learn Chinese medicine depending on his talents.

Today, one of the important tasks of a Shaolin monk is to learn to speak English and use a computer!

# What is Qi?

If you have watched the *Star Wars* movies, you already know what is *qi* because the Jedi's Force is very similar to *qi* (pronounced "chi").

As Obi-Wan Kenobi said in *Star Wars*, the Force is "an energy field created by all living things. It surrounds us, penetrates us, and binds the Galaxy together."

Simply put, *qi* is the energy that makes up the universe and is a basic idea of Chinese life. The Chinese character for *qi* means "breath" or "air" and also refers to "universal energy".

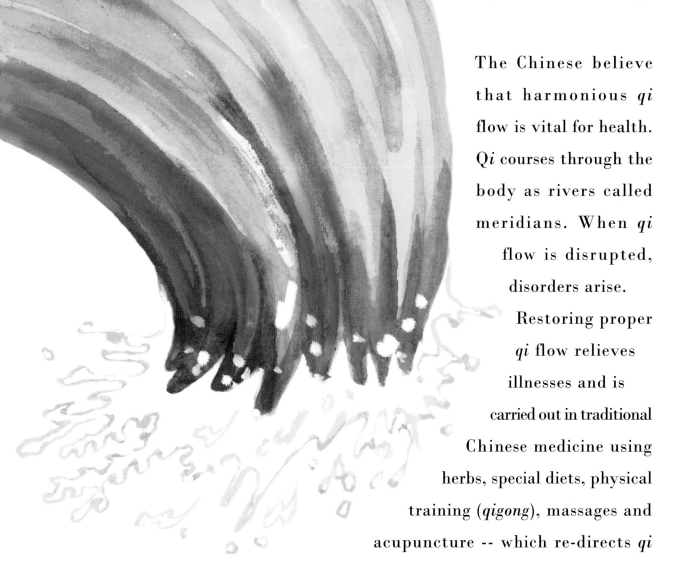

The Chinese believe that harmonious *qi* flow is vital for health. *Qi* courses through the body as rivers called meridians. When *qi* flow is disrupted, disorders arise.

Restoring proper *qi* flow relieves illnesses and is carried out in traditional Chinese medicine using herbs, special diets, physical training (*qigong*), massages and acupuncture -- which re-directs *qi* through fine needles inserted into the meridians.

What part does *qi* play in Shaolin Kung Fu? In Shaolin Kung Fu, movements are controlled by *qi* and follow circular paths. When *qi* is controlled well, movements look soft and graceful.

*Qi* is like water. A drop of water is powerless. But what on earth can stand up to the force of a tsunami? *Qi* is the same. By tapping into universal energy, one increases one's power many times over. How can an opponent hurt a kung fu master when he is unable to strike and injure a body of water?

# Amazing Shaolin Qigong

*Qigong* refers to the arts of using *qi*. The Chinese believe that *qi* resides in a place in the lower abdomen called *dan tian*.

Through breathing and body movements, *qi* can be directed to a specific part of the body, giving it tremendous power. Hence, the feet, hands and head of a Shaolin monk can smash bricks, stone blocks and wooden sticks. Even delicate parts of the body like the throat and stomach can resist weapon attacks.

This sort of *qigong* is called "hard *qigong*". The types of hard *qigong* include Iron Shirt, Scarlet Palm, Iron Head, Hard Stomach and Iron Sand Palm.

"Soft *qigong*" focuses on controlling the breathing. Practicing soft *qigong* improves blood flow and gets rid of toxins in the body. As a result, the internal organs function well and the limbs are flexible. Varieties of soft *qigong* include meditation, Eight Pieces of Brocade, and the famous *Yijinjing*, invented by Damo 1,500 years ago. *(See Dawn of Zen and Kung Fu)*

*So, how does a Shaolin disciple develop qi? Through meditation, breathing exercises and endless repetition of physical movements several hours a day for many years. To master kung fu, a Shaolin disciple must practice qigong and to master qigong, he must practice meditation!*

# Shaolin Five Animals

Dragon, snake, tiger, leopard and crane -- what pops into your mind when you think of these animals? (Yes, one of them is a mythical animal, but I'm sure you can picture it!)

Shaolin monks in their mountainous habitat saw the unique abilities of animals to survive in their natural environment. They came up with a great idea: by copying animal skills they can improve their own survival abilities.

The inventive Shaolin monks realized it was not enough to mimic the outer appearance of the animals but also the animals' inner essence. Their goal was to become One with the animals they imitated.

Whether attacking or defending, the monks achieved a profound understanding of the strong survival instincts of the animals and of their ability to adapt to nature. Such a state of oneness is only possible through the Zen practice that is part of Shaolin Kung Fu.

crane standing fast

silvery snake groping ahead

leopard looking for food

Shaolin Five Animals Kung Fu is an effective fighting art. Here are its characteristics:

Snake -- soft, circular motion with strong internal force, attacks the opponent's weak points with swift actions

Crane -- stable and tranquil on one leg, swift and elegant in action

Leopard -- emphasizes strength, great speed and momentum in attack

Dragon -- continuous and flowing motion, swerving movements in defense and attack without moving legs

Tiger -- movements are fierce and powerful, agile and elegant

golden dragon
coming out of cave

fierce tiger
coming down the mountain

# Shaolin Juvenile Kung Fu

You might have seen performances of Shaolin kids bending their limbs into mind-boggling positions and asked yourself "Now, *how did they do that?*" What you have just seen is a display of Shaolin Juvenile Kung Fu.

Juvenile Kung Fu? Is it only for kids? Yes, because boys start practicing this art at ages five or six. There is another reason it is called Juvenile Kung Fu.

After practicing this art for years the student stays as young as a child even though his hair may be white as a crane's feathers. Juvenile Kung Fu makes his body soft as cotton, light as a swallow and hard as steel. What is amazing is that a person who practices it stays as strong and sharp when he is sixty as when he was sixteen. Hence, to become a great Shaolin Kung Fu master, it is vital to learn Juvenile Kung Fu.

Young boys selected for this training must be lean and have good bone structure and flexibility. (Bigger boys are selected for Shaolin hard *qigong* training.) Basic training involves a lot of leaping and rolling. At advanced levels, the boys bend and stretch their limbs at impossible angles with soft and powerful *qi*-controlled movements. Their joints and tendons become strong and flexible. They have excellent blood and *qi* flow. And they show precise posture and fantastic power in their kung fu.

# Weapons of Shaolin

Throughout Chinese history, Shaolin disciples are well known for their skills in using a **long fighting stick** called a staff. They wield the staff with the full force of the body and strike dozens of people one after another with **blinding speed!** *(see website)*

Legend has it that 1045 years ago, Zhao Kuangyin, a Shaolin disciple, used his staff to defeat his enemies and found the Song Dynasty (960 – 1367 AD). (Of course he had lots of soldiers to help him!)

The Song Emperor's staff was **broken into two** during combat. Instead of throwing it away, he joined it together with a chain to form a sweeper -- so called because it sweeps away your opponents. Its Japanese name *nunchaku* (two-sectional staff) is well known thanks to **Bruce Lee**, who used it with devastating effect in his films to dispose of his challengers!

Shaolin weapons are divided into *long weapons* (long spear, staff, broad-sword), *short weapons* (dagger, saber), *soft weapons* (iron-chained ball), *rare weapons* (sickle, Dharma Staff) and *hidden weapons* (flying darts).

*Did you know that no other martial arts in the world boasts more types of weapons than Shaolin Kung Fu?*

# Story of Thirteen Shaolin Monks

*Did you know that almost 1,400 years ago, thirteen Shaolin monks played a big part in the founding of the Tang Dynasty, the most prosperous period in Chinese history?*

In the year 618 AD, warlord Li Simin led his troops into Luoyang (in today's Henan province) to defeat his rival Wang Shicheng. Unfortunately, Li was captured in an ambush and imprisoned in Luoyang.

Thirteen Shaolin monks led by Tanzhong decided to rescue Li. In the still of the night, they scaled the city walls and located the heavily guarded prison. Tanzhong left a few monks behind and the rest overpowered the guards and entered the prison.

Later, Li's army together with 500 monks from Shaolin finally defeated Wang and Li ascended the throne as Emperor Taizhong of the new Tang Dynasty (618 – 960 AD). Shaolin was awarded forty acres of land. Tanzhong was appointed General and led a 500-strong army in service of the emperor.

Quickly, they found Li's cell. Tanzhong carried the injured Li on his back and they fought their way out of the prison and through the city gates.

The party had not escaped far before Wang's soldiers on horseback caught up with them. Using only their staffs, the thirteen monks clashed with hundreds of soldiers! Suddenly from nowhere, Li's rescue troops appeared and routed Wang's soldiers. The thirteen monks and Li were saved!

**From 1911 to Present**

Shaolin Temple was burnt by Kuo Ming Tang (KMT) army soldiers (1928). The fire lasted 40 days.

Bruce Lee invented *Jeet Kune Do* (1960s).

Popular *Kung Fu* TV series in U.S starring David Carradine showed an imagined Shaolin Temple (1970s).

Bruce Lee died (1973). His last film *Enter the Dragon*, was released after his death and changed American cinema.

The film *Shaolin Temple* starring Jet Li ignited a new wave of interest in kung fu within China and a following in the West (1979).

Shaolin Temple was restored. Shaolin monks started touring Western countries giving kung fu performances. The Chinese government promoted the study of martial arts as a sport called *wushu* (martial arts) (1980s).

Ang Lee's *Crouching Tiger, Hidden Dragon* became the most successful foreign film in the U.S and won four Oscars (2000).

| | |
|---|---|
| **2,800 years ago (800 BC)** | Beginnings of Chinese boxing. |
| **2,500 years ago (527 BC)** | Siddhartha Gautama became "Buddha". |
| **1,784 years ago**<br>**(Warring States 221 – 617 AD)** | Construction of Shaolin Temple (495 AD). Damo founded *Chan* (Zen) school of Buddhism (527 AD). |
| **1,387 years ago**<br>**(Tang Dynasty 618 – 960 AD)** | Li Simin was rescued by Shaolin monks and became Tang Emperor. A new Shaolin Temple was built in southern Fujian Province (683 AD). |
| **1,045 years ago**<br>**(Song Dynasty 960 – 1276 AD)** | Zhao Kuangyin, a Shaolin disciple, founded the Song Dynasty. Martial artists all over China came to Shaolin. New kung fu styles, such as *Eagle's Claw*, were created. |
| **745 years ago**<br>**(Yuan Dynasty 1260 – 1368 AD)** | Mongol rulers forbade martial arts practice but the Chinese trained secretly. |
| **637 years ago**<br>**(Ming Dynasty 1368 – 1644 AD)** | *Praying Mantis* was founded by a Shaolin Master, Wang Lang (1627 AD). Shaolin monks fought Japanese pirates on the southern coast of China. |
| **361 years ago**<br>**(Qing Dynasty 1644 – 1911 AD)** | Many schools of Shaolin martial arts thrived. Southern Shaolin Temple became the meeting place for rebels planning to overthrow the Qing government. Qing armies burned the temple. |

*A Musical Journey: from the Great Wall of China to the Water Towns of Jiangnan*, by Liow Kah Joon

*An American Booksellers Association Book Sense Children's Pick Autumn 2004*

"This book has great colorful pictures for kids and is written in a way that kids will find it interesting. It's hard to cram so many years of Chinese history into a short children's book but the author has done a good job of hitting the interesting high points. The accompanying CD has some wonderful original compositions. This is a welcome addition to the library of children's books on China." — Kristian Ball, Families of the China Moon, Richmond VA, USA

"*A Musical Journey* guides readers through the regions of China in an artistic, informative, and fun way. Each region is described in prose and through a beautiful painting, a song, and an illustration of a child wearing the local folk costume." — Leigh Ann Johnson, University Book Store, Seattle, WA, USA

For more information about *A Musical Journey* go to

# www.living-chinese-symbols.com